WHAT IS OWED THE DEAD

POEMS BY
R. H. W. DILLARD

ALSO BY R. H. W. DILLARD

POETRY
> The Day I Stopped Dreaming About Barbara Steele (1966)
> News of the Nile (1971)
> After Borges (1972)
> The Greeting: New & Selected Poems (1981)
> Just Here, Just Now (1994)
> Sallies (2001)

FICTION
> The Book of Changes (1974)
> The First Man on the Sun (1983)
> Omniphobia (1995)

CRITICISM
> Horror Films (1976)
> Understanding George Garrett (1988)

TRANSLATIONS
> Plautus's The Little Box [Cistellaria] (1995)
> Aristophanes' The Sexual Congress [Ecclesiazusae] (1999)

WHAT IS OWED THE DEAD

POEMS BY R. H. W. DILLARD

> By understanding I understand diligence
> and attention, appropriately understood
> as actuated self-knowledge, a daily acknowledgement
> of what is owed the dead.
>
> *Geoffrey Hill*

Published by Factory Hollow Press

Factory Hollow Press
Amherst, Massachusetts

www.factoryhollowpress.com

Design by Pam Glaven, Impress, Northampton, MA
Printed by The Studley Press, Dalton, MA

ISBN 0-9840698-8-0
Copyright © 2011 by R. H. W. Dillard

To the memory of George Garrett

*Nether did he doute of the promes of God
through vnbeliefe,
but was strengthened in ye faith,
& gaue glorie to God.*

ACKNOWLEDGEMENTS

Grateful acknowledgement is made to the following publications in which some of the poems herein first appeared, sometimes with different titles and in slightly different form:

The Album: "Passion," "Passion 2," "Passion 3"
Blackbird: An Online Journal of Literature and the Arts: "Afterword," "Canto," "Correlative," "Courage," "Exile," "Exile 2," "Light," "Requiem," "Sheep," "Visions"
The Hollins Critic: "Fly," "Raven"
James Dickey Review: "Fame," "Fame 2"
1913: a journal of forms: "Byzantium," "Daemon," "Dance," "Eros," "Naked," "Old Song," "Poetry," "Wind," "Yawp"
NOÖ Weekly: "Fire," "Howl"
The Richmond Style Weekly: "Satyricon," "Satyricon 2"
Shenandoah: The Washington and Lee University Review: "Next War," "Next War 2," Next War 3," "Next War 4," "Next War 5"
Southern Quarterly: "Dust"
The four lines on the title page are from Geoffrey Hill's *The Triumph of Love* (Boston, New York: Houghton Mifflin, 1998) p. 63.
The lines in the "Epilogue" are from George Barker's *The Dead Seagull* (London: John Lehmann, 1950) pp. 126-127.

I would also like to acknowledge the kindness and support of those of my friends, poets all, who read these poems and encouraged their author as they were being written, especially George Garrett who continually made suggestions and urged me on, Jeanne Larsen, Kelly Cherry, Dara Wier, Annie Dillard, and my sternest as well as most supportive critic, Duffie Taylor; to the editors, most of them poets as well, who were kind enough to publish many of these poems, Renee Branum, Jack Christian, Casey Clabough, Sandra Doller, Greg Donovan, Rozanne Epps, Mary Flinn, Cathryn Hankla, Liana Quill, Allison Seay, R. T. Smith, and William Wright; to everyone at Factory Hollow Press; and, of course, to George Barker (1913-1991), whom I never met but who became the guiding spirit of this entire enterprise.

CONTENTS

Raven – 1
Canto – 2
Tristia – 3
Fly – 4
Visions – 5
Next War – 6
Anxiety – 7
Old Song – 8
Satyricon – 9
Satyricon 2 – 10
Howl – 11
Fire Sermon – 12
Correlative – 13
Bird Girl – 14
Memory – 15
Afterword – 16
Eros – 17
Oblivion – 18
Am – 19
Sheep – 20
Fame – 21
Geography – 22
Requiem – 23
Exile – 24
Exile 2 – 25
Yawp – 26
Naked – 27

Disaster – 28
Daemon – 29
Barfly – 30
Next War 2 – 31
Next War 3 – 32
Waking – 33
Next War 4 – 34
Wind – 35
Dance – 36
Next War 5 - 37
Byzantium – 38
Fame 2 – 39
Fire – 40
Courage – 41
Dust – 42
Light – 43
Fire 2 – 44
Doubt – 45
Exile 3 – 46
Poetry – 47
Night – 48
Exile 4 – 49
Passion – 50
Passion 2 – 51
Passion 3 - 52
Epilogue - 53

WHAT IS OWED THE DEAD

RAVEN

Edgar, they are still telling lies about you,
Old calumnies, scornful, never-ending,
(The drink, the dope), humdrum, lollygags,
Starved your mother-in-law to death
Though fully known Mrs. Clemm alive
And well when they did you in in Baltimore,
Suppose some solace in that you're not
The only one they victimize these days,
All those lies, caw caw cacophony,
Smear the air like mustered crows,
Is that what it all amounts to, crowbait,
Glassy eyes, those "windows to the soul"
Cracked by hungry beaks, midday
Snack? better to lie there in Baltimore
Than to have to put up with lies, more lies,
Lies within lies, and "all within the *Spirit Divine*."

EDGAR ALLAN POE: "The Philosophy of Composition," *Eureka*
VLADIMIR NABOKOV: *Lolita*

CANTO

Granted, Ez, Monticello's stables are nice
To visit, wouldn't want to live there, but then
Spent no time in open cell or closed tent
Either, "Caged Eagle," old buzzard, lamenting, γύψ,
Your "twice-crucified" dead, chthonic tonic,
"H., M." among the strewn corpses, the stench,
Mussolini poem was lost when the hard drive
Crashed, no great loss, always another sawed-off
Little Caesar around, *hic*, "Mother of God,"
Blacksmith's spawn, *rusticus* ready
To fill the air with deception and betrayal,
Kiss the current *Führer*'s furry arse, that part
Of the job apparently not too difficult,
"Is this the end?" why is it, do you think,
That the silence of those final years rings truer
Than so much of all that village explaining?

EZRA POUND: "Canto XXVIII"
W. R. BURNET: *Little Caesar*

TRISTIA

Black page, Laurie, marbled, alas,
Fractal, seldom understood, "dark veil"
Or "motly emblem," still "mystically hid,"
All do, you know, know, everyone the same,
Yet each unique, slow fall of snowflakes
Down the brick wall, excited, "Life not death,"
Fifteen year old girl (05/22/2001), first contacts,
World suddenly "so full of a number of things,"
In focus, so interesting, "the great adventure."
All, yes, "a COCK and a BULL," but even while
You were coughing it up, knew blood
Is the life, not death, "glorious" only
To one undead, that sudden need to leave
For France, Valima, Caribbean,
Tuberculosis, tuberculosis, peritonitis,
Aes triplex, loud, alive, "ten times in a day."

LAURENCE STERNE: *The Life and Opinions of Tristram Shandy, Gentleman*
SHERWOOD ANDERSON: epitaph, Marion, Virginia
ROBERT LOUIS STEVENSON: "Aes Triplex"
GARRETT FORT: screenplay, Tod Browning's *Dracula*

FLY

"Some bright morning," John, having "seen
The dawn erupt," depart, "skulled ghost,"
Longtime gatherer of the dead, "crow . . .
Mockingbird . . . cardinals," tenderly tied
Bursts of feather, flies, delicate display, dome
Popped once, then again, like a lost child's
Squib, (06/13/2007), day you died, unlucky,
Lucky, nearly drowned, nearly frozen, punched
Shoulder-deep in snow, simple gravity, simple loss,
In water, by water, "now where do you look?"
Who once taught poets to walk, "safe to stand,"
On water, "on ice," "dead birch tree on the shore,"
"God's celestial shore," scars (02/02/1996) scratched,
Spiked snow tires, steep drive, so determined, still there,
"Bear witness" you were here, yet "this world . . . over,"
No "red flag," no need to stay, only need, to "fly away."

JOHN ENGELS: "At Dawn on Gun Point," "The House of the Dead,"
"Bird Song," "That Day," "Signals from the Safety Coffin"
NORBERT ENGELS AND JOHN ENGELS: *Writing Techniques*
A. E. BRUMLEY: "I'll Fly Away"
DARA WIER: "A Border State Sees Its Coldest Season"

VISIONS

"Not a search for God," alone on the train,
"Railroads of the Night," (10/22/1959), reading
Mexico City Blues, twenty-two, not digging it,
Didn't know enough, dumb as a pig, nightfall,
Car crowded, Sweet Briar girls strut the aisles,
Hang over seat backs, bare thighs, "poor girls,
Did they always want attention?" sitting, exile,
Next seat, smashed thumb, red wine shared,
Bottle in a twisted paper bag, friends shot down
In a Budapest street (he got away), Soviet tank,
"God in search of a human being," you, too,
Jaqui Keracky, navel hernia, ομφαλός,
The taped silver dollar, "a very lonely guy,"
Kallaquack, "Mother of God, is this the end?"
Remember, Brother Jack, "nobody's alone,"
Canuck, Hunky, self, "for more than a minute."

JACK KEROUAC: *Mexico City Blues*
STELLA KEROUAC: Interview (10/21/1969)
W. R. BURNET: *Little Caesar*

NEXT WAR

Dark early morning, (11/04/1918), the Sambre,
Canal bank, very heavy fire, pontoons shell
Shattered, trying to cross, a raft, and then,
"The old Lie," you, Wilfred, hit and hit ● ● ●
The Great War, "five healthy girls died of fright,"
French village, British barrage, "in one night,"
And always another war — 1944, dad, Captain, USAAF,
Pedaling an English bike, V-1 sputters, glides, explodes,
Buzz bomb, doodlebug, in the ditch, "This one's," triage,
"A dead one," always choices, always, attacks, betrayal,
November 1918, day by day 2,088 die, no point,
"By choice they made themselves immune,"
For what? Dryburgh, Haig's grave, single cut stone,
Simple wooden cross, wreaths, wreaths, wreaths
Of red paper poppies (06/28/1987), "to pity and whatever
Mourns," father survived, "*pro patria*," you did not.

    Wilfred Owen: "Dulce Et Decorum Est," Letter (10/29/1918),
      "Insensibility"

ANXIETY

Today as then, "divided days," forced
To "choose from ways, all of them evil,
One," border crossings, lies, lies, lies,
Wystan, you fled NYC, mugged in Oxford,
Never ends, remembering once a voice
Through morning mail slot, "O all the instruments
Agree," years later, hearing older lady to friend,
You, reading (03/21/1972), intoning, "I thought,"
Greatest hits, one last appearance in US,
Wrinkled, slippered, lionized, "he was going
To read poetry," even now, words about love,
"About suffering," just stew for the pot,
"Emptied of its poetry," scholarly pissing
In the kitchen sink, you scrawled name over
OED, tagging, and yet always seemed aware
That "goodness," lately or early, "is timeless."

W. H. AUDEN: *Paid on Both Sides*, "In Memory of W. B. Yeats,"
   "Musée des Beaux Arts," "Archaeology"

OLD SONG

"What do I know of poetry," you once asked,
"Among so many definitions?" openly doubtful,
Unsure of "high-hung laurel terraces your heart
So hankered for," and for Gene Derwood, too, "wild
Eyes . . . that funny hat," loving husband, trying, trying,
One by each in *Great Poems*, three each in *Immortal*,
"Best anthologist," but, like "mr u," less than demure,
Pocket Book of Modern Verse (04/1954), so important,
Little Treasury of Modern Poetry (06/22/1956), read,
Thumbed, reread, so much not yet understood, desired,
Always at hand, "as if forever," all those chosen ones,
Young scholar, your kind arrangement, after interview
With Barker, your NYC apartment, you, as she left,
Saying, "sad man of ashes," through the slowly
Closing hallway door, "Remember, I'm a poet, too,"
What, Oscar, "perplexed, voiceless," do you now know?

OSCAR WILLIAMS: "Autobiographical Note," "On Meeting a Stranger in a Bookshop"
GEORGE BARKER: "Formal Elegy on the Death of Oscar Williams"
GEORGE GARRETT: "Anthologies II (Here and Now)"
E. E. CUMMINGS: "mr u will not be missed"
ROBERT LOWELL: Review in *The Sewanee Review*

SATYRICON

"*Arma, cruor, caedes, incendia,*" yes, Arbiter,
Same old story, tale of, well, not love, gory
Doings, battle, blood, slaughter, fire, whole
Shebang, "*totaque bella ante oculos volitant,*"
Eyes bloody red, what they daily see,
Emperor off at villa, chopping cottonwood
On ranch, war, rumors of war, distant, but
Now with body bags, mercenaries or
At least the poor, no choice, more of them
Every day, while the rich, okay, the rich,
Surely, always with us, let sick heal sick,
Poor pack ERs, "deeper in debt," circuses,
Makeovers on every TV tube, "reality,"
Poetry, all arts debased, while everything
Is "art," Britney proclaims her art, shake it,
Shake it, "*pecuniae cupiditas,*" you said it.

PETRONIUS ARBITER: *Satyricon*
MERLE TRAVIS: "Sixteen Tons"

SATYRICON 2

Sound familiar, Mr. P, whole damned
Thing? Not much difference twixt
Now, then? Love of money, yes,
Burn cities down entire, people
Too, makes things a little nicer for
The rich, "always with you," chew
Our corpses to get what small change
We have, masticate the bloody cud,
No problem, swallow, no remorse,
Lichas as simpering bride, Fellini, yes,
But true enough to you, gay wedding,
Angry crowd outside, don't notice
What the rich, behind them, are up
To, always with us: "*Quisquis habet
Nummos*," you got the cash, "*secura
Navigat aura*," the wind is at your back.

Petronius Arbiter: *Satyricon*
Federico Fellini and Bernardino Zapponi: *Satyricon*
The Gospel According to St. Mark 14:7

HOWL

William Blake, Walt, then you, Allen,
Chanting "best minds . . . destroyed,"
Crazy Mama's boy, "screaming bugs
Of Mussolini," H. too, naked, "con man
Extraordinaire," cranking the harmonium,
Such a sweet voice, "What is this life?"
Talked professor into *Howl*, (03/27/1958),
Fourth Printing, 75¢, shocked classmate,
"Hey, this guy is queer!" lion always
At the window ("Not this time Baby"),
No Albanian howls for you "except in an urn
Of ashes," no surprise, "die when you die,"
But well off, not like lone Jack, 3-piece suit,
At the end, lion "back again," last word
Not yours, never is, only cheap newspaper
Headline, "Beat Poet to 'Howl' No More."

Allen Ginsberg: "Howl," "Kaddish," "The Lion for Real,"
  "Things I'll Not Do (Nostalgias)," "Gospel Noble Truths"
Bob Dylan: blurb, AG, *Collected Poems 1947-1980*
Headline, *The Roanoke Times*, April 6, 1997

FIRE SERMON

"Slowly the poison," that voice through mail slot
Again, Bill, not your "sad, snarly voice," drunk,
Hung over, dumb as pork, "whole bloodstream
Fills," mockery, "the pain, it is the pain endures,"
Your cross words puzzled out, "irrotational"
Then stopped, "don't want madhouse
And the whole thing there," how close
To madness, often are, so far from love,
Breaking off mid-lecture to sit down, briefcase,
Exchange white socks, resume, eyes bright,
Those round round glasses, later big mustache,
Beard draped below chin like furbelow, Old Man
Marx, Milton, Will, your rage at Christ, "waste
Remains and kills," notes longer than poems,
Bhikku, at last love lost at last, so what
To do, you knew, "best thing to be up and go."

WILLIAM EMPSON: "Missing Dates," "Villanelle," "Bacchus,"
    "Let it go," "Aubade"

CORRELATIVE

Regnant, your "magistracy," Tom, demanded, so far
From Mississip, "strong brown god," to Thames, show me,
Through glasses, down distinctive nose, Anglo, "pubs
Being open," Christmas, "till midnight," clerk, then, publisher,
Then, "time present," E. P., whom you owed much, stiff
Salute, "DUCE," honored, you, "*decaduto*," vilified,
"Apeneck" critics de(con)struct, unmoving words: *racist
Royalist anti-semite wife-crushing rotter*, wonder if they
"Have understood a word" you wrote, "hoo hoo hoo,"
Bird in rose garden, *close reading, only fifties Cold War
Cover-up*, O. P., "loved bad jokes," limp with laughter,
Dame Edith, whoopee cushion, *sexist, piggy,* "effanineffable,"
Yet defined wasted century, "Marie, hold on tight. And down
We went," T. S., all those initials from you, F. T., W. H., e. e.,
Pell mell, if you're right "time past" is "present in time future,"
Then hope remains, "all manner of thing shall be well."

T. S. Eliot: "The Cultivation of Christmas Trees," *Four Quartets*
   ("Burnt Norton," "The Dry Salvages," "Little Gidding"),
   "Sweeney Among the Nightingales," "Fragment of an Agon,"
   "The Naming of Cats," *The Waste Land*
Ezra Pound: "Canto LXXVIII"
George Barker: "Elegiacs for T. S. Eliot"

BIRD GIRL

"Big and solemn," William, you saw ravens,
"Nature not cruel," exiled, Eden to England,
"Merely indifferent," birds, *criollo*, not dogs,
Only distinction, they roll in shit, metaphysical
Thoughts, *"siempre lo interrumpió la felicidad,"*
By happiness, Bird Girl, "Rima of the mind," high
Overhead, flowing through leaves, flitting
Sunlight, not other sort of runic Rima, sideshow
Bird Girl, too many of those today, "Gooble
Gobble," theory, queer, moribund, "solemn and
Big," overlook gauchos, dreams, lost green mansions,
"Hey, Koo Koo," croak, flutter, strut, "give
Somebody else a chance," Rima's "words when
Spoke reflected . . . despair," all ruins, ash, cinder,
Snake's mark, Rima, *"sin vos,"* without you, *"y siu
Dios,"* or God, *"y mi,"* what forgiveness now?

W. H. HUDSON: *Birds and Man, Green Mansions*
JORGE LUIS BORGES: *"Sobre The Purple Land"*
TOD BROWNING: *Freaks*

MEMORY

Now, Julie, at last, you know "what kingdoms
Come," farewells past, wary to the end, but took
Too long, who, like Adam, knew the names
Of things so well, "lilac, forsythia, orange,
Sharon rose," whom T. R. taught bone's dance,
In turn so many taught to sing that tune,
Argued with Wordsworth, also everyone else,
Old crank, plagued by demon alcohol, older,
More dangerous demons, too, led hurt, wounded
Young into that dark, "You are a poet," once
To bright student, "God help you," but did not,
Injured yourself, know how deep the shadow
Cast, so smart, unaware, tough, ambitious, then
Told by editor, too old, poetry is for the young,
Yet hard lines, bare words, incantatory, strong,
Those poems remain, alone, God help you, yes.

JULIA RANDALL: "To William Wordsworth from Virginia," "For T. R., 1908-1963," "A Winter Gallery"
THEODORE ROETHKE: "The Waking," "I Knew a Woman"

AFTERWORD

"So happiness," Frank, "and sadness," you said,
"Mix here," and "everything in old age can sadden,"
But broke down early, five, mother forbade games,
Thus books, "so make all things clear," then war,
DUCE on broken Italian walls, home, UK, then
Known, one poem in *Oxford English Verse*, one
In *Twentieth Century Modern*, but always there
And here, your edged, proud term, "Outsider,"
Not like those kids in Gorran Haven, "We're outsiders,"
Pleading, "Let us in," not really in, you, ever,
Except somewhat in USA, "this country, its laws
Of glass," taken up, later on, clambering with love over
Stony flooded Cascades in Virginia (03/1984), always
"The attempt to wake," poetry, "and breathe," you,
"And be," who knew, "because to love is frightening,"
How easy it is to choose "the freedom of our crimes."

F. T. PRINCE: "The Yüan Chên Variations II," "Walks in Rome I, IV,"
    "Not a *Paris Review* Interview," "Soldiers Bathing"
JOHN ASHBERY: "America"
COLIN WILSON: *The Outsider*

EROS

"Only on absence," philosopher notes, "in
Absence," distant lover "dreams distance gone,"
Your, Frank's, sweet "wish there were a passage
Underground that led by magic," yearning so,
"To your house," "true love," "and bed," to "sing
Together," you, Ted, "sing mouth to mouth," "can
Find no rest," "that the most overpowering passions
Thrive," "that my love were in my arms," "my suete
Leof, mi blis," your, Edna's, wry ironies, "sweet
Love, sweet thorn," so far, so near, "loved you
Wednesday," or "would have loved you in a day
Or two," your, George's, hot guilt, "love me today,"
Burnt love, "nine-tiered tigress," blind eyes of love,
"In the cage of sex," that do not see, "we remove
Our blindfolds," yet see, "so wisely and so well,"
Beyond, "suete lemmon," "burden of this joy," repair.

UMBERTO ECO: "On Symbolism"
F. T. PRINCE: "Strambotti IV"
THEODORE ROETHKE: "She," "Words for the Wind 2"
ANONYMOUS: "O Western Wind"
ANONYMOUS: "Love in Spring (BM. MS. Harley 2253)"
EDNA ST. VINCENT MILLAY: "Sonnet LXXXVI," "Thursday,"
    "Sonnet IX," "The Philosopher"
GEORGE BARKER: "Third Cycle of Love Poems VIII," "True Love,
    True Love, What Have I Done?", "Love Me Today," "Secular Elegies V,"
    "Villa Stellar XXXVI"

OBLIVION

"I am going," you said, Philip, at last, "to the inevitable,"
Looking for it, "inch-thick specs," from the beginning,
"Desire of oblivion," fucked up if not by "your mum
And dad," by something, "solving emptiness that lies
Just under," toad's eye view, "all we do," dreading,
"Get stewed," dawn, day closer to death, "near," or
What K. A. called "close," wouldn't let go, pinched,
"Cheap," American word, loving drums, the old jazz,
Hating anything new, "Parker, Pound or Picasso,"
"Movement" only fear of movement, "life," you said,
"First boredom, then fear," of "nippers" with "their
Shallow violent eyes," get to tell stories, your own, after
You've gone, M. A. did, knew trees "begin afresh,
Afresh" but knew cut grass dies, knew "we should be
Kind," but, so tight, so self-deprived, "so *ugly*," so
Praised, popular, yet knew "most things are never meant."

PHILIP LARKIN: "A Study of Reading Habits," "Wants," "This Be The
   Verse," "Ambulances," *All What Jazz*, "Dockery and Son," "Self's the Man,"
   "How," "The Trees," "The Mower," "Going, Going"
MARTIN AMIS: *Experience: A Memoir*
KINGSLEY AMIS: *Memoirs*
ROBERT FRASER: *The Chameleon Poet: A Life of George Barker*

AM

"I am," you asked, John, yes, John, John Clare,
Seeker of nests, nestlings, eggs, seasons, always
Seasons passing, repeating, eagerly, poems
Unchecked, even in darkest times, "Mind Is Dark
And Fathomless," like trapped badger, "baited
Badger tame as hog," said "feel I am," then
"Only know I am," sadness, "Alone in," isolate,
"Loneliness," seasons pass unfelt, "oh fucking
Loneliness," yet speaking loss, "None cares
Or knows," John Clare, now recognized, sadly
No Prozac, Zoloft, Lexapro for you, now known,
Oh yes, "that sweet man, John Clare," asserted
"God is every where," addressed "honest John"
As though another, nested now in letters, words,
Caring, "pigs sleep in the sty," winter, spring,
"Old cock robin," John, summer, fall and all.

    JOHN CLARE: "I Am," "Child Harold 6," "The Badger," "Sonnet: I Am,"
        "Know God is every where," "To John Clare"
    DUFFIE TAYLOR: "The Word/the word"
    THEODORE ROETHKE: "Heard in a Violent Ward"

SHEEP

Caedmon's dream (c. 658-680), herdsman, alone
In outer dark, necessary angel's command, neither wrote
Nor read (nor sung, left hall in shame), heben til hrofe,
Roofed only by heaven, praised hefaenricaes uard,
Great God, heaven's shepherd, "first English Christian
Poet," not first poetic shepherd, Theocritus, ὢ ποιμή,
Centuries (c. 270 BCE) before, contenders, love's lamenters,
Unlike you, not really herders, only "got up as poets
In farmer suits," thoughts muffled in wool, thick tufts caught
By wind and wire, Skye (06/24/1987), Virgil, too (39 BCE),
"*Tu modo nascenti puero*," pastoral prophecy or just more
Wool gathering, shipped sheep, "sniffed, poor things, for their
Green fields," cry, fall ill, one by one by one, die, wooly
Bundles, mere mutton, and yet, drowsy herdsman, you heard
"That great shepherd of the sheep," love's continuing
Demand, "feed my lambs," no doubt, "feed my sheep."

CAEDMON: "Caedmon's Hymn"
THEOCRITUS: "Thyrsis"
DAVID SLAVITT: *The Eclogues of Virgil*
VIRGIL: *Eclogues IV*
W. H. DAVIES: "Sheep"
The Epistle of Paul the Apostle to the Hebrews 13:20
The Gospel According to Saint John 21:15-16

FAME

You wanted it, Emily, glory, fame, "if fame
Belonged to me," yet didn't know how to play
The game, "could not escape her," wrote, wrote,
356 poems one year (1862), vision, pain, passion,
Stitched poems, gnomic, later wore only white,
Locked in your room, "all I have to bring to-day,"
Where tourists come and go, climb stairs, peer out,
"This, and my heart beside," dull teacher chalks up
LESBIAN AFFAIR, SISTER-IN-LAW, COPY, MEMORIZE FOR
TEST, thus "Wild nights!" safely codified, tamed,
Railroad gray pre-dawn (01/11/1960), felt, *got*, "certain
Slant of light," minor depression, you knew, Emily,
Fame "within my reach . . . could have touched,"
Bolted door, not even "approbation of my dog,"
Then "he kindly stopped," death, lonely "little
Cottage," fame, 1,775 poems, glory, "called back."

EMILY DICKINSON: poems: 26, 90, 249, 258, 712, 1743; letters: June 8, 1862; May 14, 1886

GEOGRAPHY

Worcester, Great Village, Key West, Paris,
Rio, nearby Petrópolis, Ouro Préto, islands,
Continents, water (rivers, the sea) north & south,
Your slow movements, Elizabeth, "ghostlike,"
Like those of the giant snail, "impression
Of mysterious ease," concealment even
In limpid air, "a cry of pain that could," in
Check, "have got loud and worse," loss,
Estrangement, "but hadn't," depression,
Another drink, "infinities of islands, islands,"
Mastered "art of losing," made "splendid
And curious works," finally did not lose
"Little that we get for free," geography,
Wasp's nest, "not much," rooster's crow,
"Little of our earthly trust," enisled, caught
Up, enshelled, gathering, measured motion.

ELIZABETH BISHOP: "Rainy Season; Sub-Tropics: Giant Snail,"
    "In the Waiting Room," "Crusoe in England," "One Art," "Poem"
JAMES MERRILL: Review, *The Washington Post Book World*

REQUIEM

Yes, it continues, Anna, tyranny, oppression,
Repression, recited legalisms, "This is not
A threat," illegal trials, truncheons, the knout,
Worse, of course, much worse, if not here,
There, if not there, eventually here, you knew
Behind pig's flat blank eye, look of stupid
Noncomprehension, pig's brain always thinking
Of slop, the sty, act of betrayal, evil alliance,
"Executioner's feet," slaughter, of the innocent,
The dear, Mandalstam, убийство, of the duped,
Babel, казнь, Mayakovsky's loud future,
Самоубийство, mass graves, lost masses,
Licked that satanic, Сталин, arse yourself
To save son, ГУЛаг, asked in prison line,
"Can you describe this?" you answered,
In devastation, да, yes, must, will, did, can.

Anna Akhmatova: "Requiem"
George Orwell: *Animal Farm*

EXILE

Loneliness, you, Ovid, on the Black Sea, *Pontus
Euxinus*, year 8, exiled, imperial claim, for love,
Ars Amatoris, Nelly, 1940, safe in Sweden
From Nazis but not from *die Blicke*, glances,
Der Toten, of millions going up in black
Smoke, Joseph, 1972, you, safe, too, in U. S. A.,
"*persona non grata in terra incognita*," behind
All of you, landscape, pines, lindens, aspens,
Those faces, most of all, language, "*vix
Subeunt ipsi verba Latina mihi*," old words
"Rusty and stiff," intoned (04/01/75) Russian
Verse, few understanding, sleeves rolled up,
Cigarette poised so carefully on filter,
Joseph, hand on shoulder, to shy student poet,
New room, new world, пустота, emptiness,
"Don't be," exile's best advice, "nervous."

Publius Ovidius Naso: *Tristia*, V, vii
David R. Slavitt: *The Tristia of Ovid*
Nelly Sachs: "You onlookers"
Joseph Brodsky: "Abroad," "December 24, 1971"

EXILE 2

Old Ovid, wrote home, sad complaint, *Tristia*,
Wet weather, cold, those hairy men, begging,
Ex Ponto, forgiveness, return, but no return
For you, thousands, millions, the Bantu here, other
Side of town (06/30/2005), extracted, killing ground,
Planted here, across street, Evergreen Burial Park,
Отечество, grandparents, parents, then, soon or late,
Carved stone awaits, place of final exile, abode,
The Bantu, beans, "JESUS SAVES," hand to mouth,
Like you, Nelly, know "*ein Fremder hat immer,*"
Always stranger, strange land, like an orphan,
"*Seine Heimat im Arm,*" home held close,
Even in chimneys' shadow, clutched like Zohar,
And words, letters, sounds, looted, switched,
Mystic's wisdom, all is exile away from light,
Nervous or not, afraid, in darkness, exile, always.

PUBLIUS OVIDIUS NASO: *Tristia*, V, vii
JOSEPH BRODSKY: "Anno Domini"
NELLY SACHS: "Someone comes"

YAWP

You know, Walt, Ginsberg, fifty years ago, tried,
California supermarket, "eyeing the grocery boys,"
To pin you down, afraid death not "as great as life,"
Feared "life is a suck and a sell," or Galway
Kinnell, used to start, temperature in roomful
Of young women (04/1973) rising, sleeves rolled,
Every reading reading from tattered L. of G.,
Good gray poet or doe-eyed young red shirt,
Like Elvis, take your pick, hair prickling on nape
Of neck hearing record, your voice, "America,"
As when (12/1969) young student poet looked up,
"Nimble ghosts wherever I look," from her book,
Saw you lolling in chair, feet propped, hole in sole
Of one shoe, always there, Walt, "in the adamant
Of Time," here, "surrounded by blatherers," held,
"Undisguised," universal, kosmic, yourself, you.

WALT WHITMAN: *Leaves of Grass* (1855), "America"
ALLEN GINSBERG: "A Supermarket in California"

NAKED

Not the way you pictured it, eh, Bogie, saw Death
With "silver birds," tip-toe, alluring, "between
The cold waves of his hair," instead, one night,
Cock-teased dimwit, two shots ● ● right in *The Sea
Around Us*, through the old ticker, blood all over,
"Naked on roller skates," King of Village, "sliding
Down into nowhere," those drowned, gassed girls,
Story told of double suicide on Pallisades, you, polite
Mississippi boy, ladies first, then, once she's dead,
Why jump, go back downtown, cadge drink, tell tale,
True or not, doesn't matter, found how life can
Replace art, wrote jazz poems, like Lindsay, sold
Poems on street, George Garrett bought, "fifty cents
A pop," Dylan Thomas once wiped your snotty nose,
Poems, novels, now forgot, only dive, crash, death,
And this, here's four bits, sad Max, go make a poem.

MAXWELL BODENHEIM: "Death," *Naked on Rollerskates*
GEORGE GARRETT: "Anthologies I (Then and There)"

DISASTER

June, 1877, you, William, felt "strange kind
Of feeling," urge to dance, "pace backwards
And forwards," like Caedmon, called, "divine
Inspiration," voice crying, "Write! Write!"
Great McGonnagall, Dundee "poet and Tragedian,"
Could not forget "first man who threw peas,"
Later, fruit, shouts, "Bad Poet," vegetables, jeers,
Undaunted, not "wee, sleekit, cow'rin'," not
"Mute inglorious," over 500,000 copies sold,
Poetic Gems, "read when Milton's P. L." long gone,
Bard of "Silvery Tay," not so (06/28/1987), dark, gray,
No whale at "sport and play," yet better poets
Every day forgot, you, once turned away, Queen's
Door, "not to think," ordered, "of coming back again,"
Such is fame, you were, are, will be, like crashed bridge,
"Remember'd," prayers answered, "for a very long time."

WILLIAM MCGONAGALL: "Brief Autobiography," "Reminiscences,"
    "The Tay Bridge Disaster," "The Famous Tay Whale"
ANONYMOUS: "Ode to William McGonagall"
ROBERT BURNS: "To a Mouse"
THOMAS GRAY: "Elegy Written in a Country Churchyard"
    Punch

DAEMON

Driven, Louise, to tell and "tell again," same story,
"Beauty and sorrow," book of "the bitter heart,"
Your complaint came hard, only 105 poems saved,
Forty-six years of exacting work, precise, "subject,"
Said Roethke, "given its due," added, "no more,"
Marianne Moore, "compactness compacted,"
Hurt and hurt, private, yet, again, again, "normal
And selfish and heartless," repeating what can
Be told, "more things move than blood," so aware,
"In the heart," a lonely aging alone, dying alone,
Fewer lines year by year, days and nights flowing,
Working in library carrel (01/1969), slipping
Slowly into sleep, sliding, soft plop, to the floor,
Librarians on ready alert, only a year to go,
Knowing "you cannot take yourself in," despite
Time's taunt, allures of love, false solace of sorrow.

LOUISE BOGAN: "The Daemon," "Betrothed," "Exhortation," "Evening in the Sanitarium," "Night," "Summer Wish"

BARFLY

Critics, Hank, you were right, still riled up,
"Always going to be there," aiming to kick,
"The useless anger of the living for the dead,"
Your "big-balled" crotch, all those fat books,
No end, those sales, those fucking websites,
Critic on make compares you to Zane Grey,
Ayn Rand, to Edgar A. Guest, for gods' sake,
Doesn't approve your BMW, or, like Clare,
Publisher patron, $100 a week just to write,
$7,000 per by the end, didn't "confess" enough,
Wanted to "be lucky *and* good," tough, bitter,
Sentimental brawler in your cups, Mahler on radio,
Writing, took last punch, cancer, writing, hustling,
Old clown, for "rightful place in Classic American
Literature," typing lineups, writers, Buk, like you,
"Those who help us," you wrote it, "get on through."

CHARLES BUKOWSKI: "The Barometer," "It's Over and Done,"
    "Before Aids," "Help Wanted and Received," "The Gods Are Good,"
    "The Feel of It"

NEXT WAR 2

"Even to dream," for you, Robert, "pain," six wounds
One day (07/20/1916), large and small, marble ● chip,
Tombstone, "foolish record of old-world fighting,"
Over eye, shell ● fragment through lung, "done
For," orders, "Men | will | lie | down," obeyed,
"Duty to run mad," obituary in *Times*, survived
Seven more decades, but asked "Is this joy?" alive
"And the others dead," dismissed as "rattle-headed"
By Bloomsbury set, knew "no escape" from trenches,
"No such thing," not even in analeptic verse, 1,202
Poems, written in "fifth dimension," eternal repetition,
"Die with a forlorn hope," slain, reborn, Sacred King,
"But soon to be raised," dreamed of Goddess, loved,
Loved by women *sans merci*, Riding, wives, Sufic
Muses, yet "wars don't change," next war, next, next,
"Nightfall," inner, "not mere failure," outer, "of daylight."

ROBERT GRAVES: "To Robert Nichols," "The Face in the Mirror," *Goodbye to All That*, "Recalling War," "The Survivor," "The Castle," "The Next War," "Green Flash"
COLIN WILSON: *Dreaming to Some Purpose*
VIRGINIA WOOLF: *The Diary of Virginia Woolf*, Volume III

NEXT WAR 3

Keith, "you're shit or bust," batman said, "you
Are," disobeying to get into it, tanks, 8th Army,
In desert, Alamein, Rommel's Afrika Korps,
Respected, Bersaglieri, "W Duce W il Re," not,
"Combined cruelty," booby traps, "with cowardice,"
Death, old poetic companion, all around, "gun
Barrels split like celery," other poets, Auden,
Huddling in NYC, Barker, back in England
Ducking bombs, duty, Wilbur, fighting, infantry,
Across Europe, Ciardi, in air over Japan, lived
On, while you, back from behind enemy lines,
"Mentioned in dispatches," younger than even
Owen, D-Day + 3, "beast on back," simplified,
● ● ● ● ● ● ● "BANG" ● ● ● ● ● ● ●
"Split the glass," bombardment, "lunatic explosive,"
"Put in the bag," lacking, you, only "time, time."

Keith Douglas: *Alamein to Zum Zum*, "Bête Noire," "I Experiment,"
"Tel Aviv," "Simplify Me when I'm Dead," "On a Return from Egypt,"
"Landscape with Figures"

WAKING

"Intrepid scholar," Ted, "of the soil," Dickey said
You "knew the big thing," but Bogan accused you
Of being "afraid to suffer," yet suffer you did,
Recurring depression, the manly cure, drink,
Sleep, "by lust alone" keeping "the mind alive,"
Surrounded by, said this to Garrett, steam bath,
Wesleyan, "all those flat young tummies," dug
Deep, the greenhouse, roses, roses, "a congress
Of stinks," always longing for "the imperishable
Quiet"— death, God, Godhead —"at the heart
Of form," but, "like a tyro," working the critics,
Afraid of T. S. E., more so "those tin-horn
Aristotelian text-creepers," then heart stopped,
Sunk into "a deeper sleep," in pool, now garden,
"Black hairy roots," where you saw, "magnified
And shimmering," finally, "what the great dead say."

THEODORE ROETHKE: "The Manifestation," "The Motion,"
　　"Root Cellar," "The Longing," "Plaint," "Weed Puller," "I Waited,"
　　"Words for the Wind," Letter to Louis Untermeyer (08/18/1961),
　　Letter to Karl Shapiro (09/08/1954)
JAMES DICKEY: *Classes on Modern Poets and the Art of Poetry*
LOUISE BOGAN: Letter to Theodore Roethke (08/23/1935)

NEXT WAR 4

Visionary like William Blake, Isaac, you, like other poet-
Painter, Keith Douglas — who said (1943) "I only repeat
What you were saying" — saw flowers bloom like lice,
Heard lark's song, met "sardonic rat," battlefields crazier
Even than childhood East End, Saucy Jack's Whitechapel
"Juwes" (09/30/1888) only two years & two months before
You lost twin brother at birth, bad luck of the Rosenbergs,
Later (1961) your sister Annie wind-blown from bridge,
Brighton, into cement mixer, your great-niece, USA, child,
Laughed, was spanked and sent to bed, this decades after,
On Western Front, denied transfer to Palestine, you, more
Fool you, volunteered (04/01/1918) to return to trenches,
Close combat, ● ● "An end!" ● ●, "dark air spurts
With fire," your body fought over for days, "burnt black
By strange decay," pray you found, like your Moses,
In that madness, some "consciousness like naked light."

ISAAC ROSENBERG: "The Immortals," "Louse Hunting," "Returning,
 We Hear the Larks," "Break of Day in the Trenches," "Dead Man's
 Dump," *Moses: A Play*
KEITH DOUGLAS: "Desert Flowers"
DONALD RUMBELOW: *Jack the Ripper: The Complete Casebook*

WIND

"O," you wrote, "westron wind," now uncertain
When or who you might have been, five, maybe,
Centuries ago, "when wyll thow blow," lonely
Query, "the smalle rayne," recited, sung, revised,
"Downe can rayne," appropriated, wind "sweet"
To Herrick, thinking of kisses, Henley, no "hope,"
Yearning, "Cryst yf my love wer in my arms,"
Yeats, at the end, "O that I were young again,"
Satirical, Dehn, "had my arms again," anti-nuke,
Fr. Raymond, "point sharper," resurrection,
"Than rain," but raked by scholars, historicized,
Condemned — Christian dead white male —
Studied, closely, structurally, culturally, queerly,
Post-colonially, deconstructed, psychoanalyzed,
Yet, assured, "and I yn my bedde agayne," poem,
Yours, as always, intact, pure, true, inviolable.

ANONYMOUS: "Westron Wind"
ROBERT HERRICK: "To the Western Wind"
WILLIAM ERNEST HENLEY: "Bring Her Again, O Western Wind"
WILLIAM BUTLER YEATS: "Politics"
PAUL DEHN: *Quake, Quake, Quake: A Leaden Treasury of Nuclear Verse*
RAYMOND ROSELIEP: "The Small Rain"

DANCE

"In old age," you wrote, Bill, "the mind casts off,"
Bought *Paterson Five* (03/18/1961), "rebelliously,"
So young, in awe, but *got* it only in theory,
"May croak at any moment," (04/25/1951) to Stevens,
"But we're not old," that's theory for you, "to theorize
Is to falsify," you knew, "reduce all things to method,"
Thus your stern dictum, "no ideas but in things,"
Could never really explain 'variable foot,' 'measure,'
Yet could show, saxifrage, plums, taught now,
Wheel barrow, to every schoolchild, not *Paterson*,
Too raw, plexed, tough, "I have seen what I have seen,"
Saw old age, bum heart, strokes, yet at sixty-seven,
"More attractive to girls than when seventeen,"
"Heel & toe," the ancient dance, "ya ho! ta ho!"
Doctor Bill, that old joke, "burden of poems," words,
Punched slowly, letter by letter, ageless, no joke.

WILLIAM CARLOS WILLIAMS: *Paterson V*, Letter to Wallace Stevens
    (04/25/1951), *In the American Grain*, "A Sort of a Song," *I Wanted to Write a Poem: The Autobiography of the Works of a Poet*, "Heel & Toe to the End," "*Paterson VI*"
DAVID PEARS: *Ludwig Wittgenstein*
ROBERT LOWELL: "William Carlos Williams"

NEXT WAR 5

General Nivelle's offensive, 600 yards gained,
130,000 casualties, five days, among the dead
First day, (04/09/1917, 7:30 a.m.), you, Edward,
Spring dawn, Arras, "mistier, farther and farther,"
Singing, home, "all the birds," nearby shell ● blast,
Trench desk, chair, pocket Shakespeare, preserved,
"House of glass," War Museum (07/05/1987), you,
"Under a foreign clod," after years of travel books,
Reviews, depressive, "black dog shakes his chain
And moans," finally freed by Frost to poems, 143
(12/1914 to 01/1917), "listening to the rain," birds,
Trees, countrymen, "words of such spirit," afraid
"May lose my way and myself," yet "when the war
Began to turn young men to dung," would not look
Or turn away, "I should prefer the truth," enlisted,
Artist's Rifles, like Owen, ● ● ●, "or nothing."

EDWARD THOMAS: "Adlestrop," "I Built Myself a House of Glass,"
    "No One Cares Less than I," "Two Houses," "Rain," "How I Began,"
    "Lights Out," "Gone, Gone Again," "The Chalk-Pit"

BYZANTIUM

"Fastened," yes, Willie, "to a dying animal," daily,
"Old bones," heartache, sad dream, each "night's
Remorse," absence, that "cold eye," your late poems,
"Words of a dead man," no, "old man looking
On life" in doubt, "in scorn," mind "perhaps too old,"
Less "rich," yet once, London days, young, "dark
And pale and tall," tagged your footsteps, shouted,
Foul ragamuffins, "DEAD MAN," you, "alone
And aware," actually pleased, but years later, worried
"Poet's labour mere rejection," longed for "passionate
And powerful syntax," found, "lonely of heart,"
Just "why an old man" should "be mad," yearning,
"Withered away," for presence, "her in my arms,"
To be "young again," sparrows "brawling in the eaves,"
But dark morning's chill, "hoo hoo hoo," discovers,
Across bed, desire only, only "shadowes shadow."

WILLIAM BUTLER YEATS: "Sailing to Byzantium," "The Black Tower,"
"The Choice," "Under Ben Bulben," *The Death of Cuchulain, A Vision,
The Autobiography of William Butler Yeats*, "The Circus Animals' Desertion,"
"A General Introduction to My Work," *The Land of Heart's Desire*,
"Why Should Not Old Men Be Mad?", "Politics," "The Sorrow of Love"
W. H. AUDEN: "In Memory of W. B. Yeats"
DOROTHY RICHARDSON: *The Trap*
T. S. ELIOT: "Fragment of an Agon"
RICHARD CRASHAW: "Act. 5. *The sicke implore* St. Peter's *shadow*"

FAME 2

Stranding you blue-faced in the oven forever,
But books everywhere, this *Ariel*, that *Ariel*, death,
Wag says, yours, Sylvia, good career move, "hyena
Aching" on every scrap you left, notebooks, diaries,
Sketches, painted hearts, "fame," you said, "will ruin
Everything," that private yearning for the "horizontal,"
Instead, "pale, slumped," linked forever — or so
It seems — to Sexton, suicide infectious, shadow cast,
Young writer (GDR, 04/1982) held students hostage,
Fired one bullet ● into ceiling, other ● into her head,
Sad friend ● followed in city park, "final grotesque
Joke," other Daddy's girl in movie played your part,
Your "brilliant tense presence" fixed, iconic, "perfected,"
"Unthinkable old despair," at end "new agony," children
Sealed apart, "coldness sifting down," no more hope,
Gassy hiss, "to 'scape the serpent's tongue,'" success.

SYLVIA PLATH: "I Am Vertical," "Dirge for a Joker," "Edge"
TED HUGHES: "The Dogs Are Eating Your Mother," "Ouija," "Visit"
ROBERT LOWELL: "Foreword" to *Ariel*
WILLIAM SHAKESPEARE: *A Midsummer Night's Dream*
RICHARD WILBUR: "Cottage Street, 1953"

FIRE

"*Ainsi je travaille,*" you wrote, Arthur, "*à me render
Voyant,*" sixteen years old, aflame, "*voleur de feu,*"
Believing yourself "*sans coeur,*" yet always, *toujours*,
Always, victimized by "*l'interminable ennui,*" bored
Into speech, then, eighteen, out again, into vast moving
Silence, Verlaine's bullet ● in your wrist, "*la vielle
Ironie, l'Amour,*" driven into desert, scorched, seared,
"Tortured, transcendent-striving will," 8 kilos, gold,
Slung around your waist, "*ca me flanque la dysenterie,*"
Shitting money at "Rainbow's" end, Quilty's cheap joke,
Other joke, academic building honored your biographer,
Re-named (04/21/2006) for cash, *l'université d'argent*,
Ransacked hell for "*langage universel*," ran slaves, guns,
Always motion, "*inouï,*" but interred "*imagination,*" art,
Then one leg, "*Pourquoi,*" asked, "*donc existons-nous?*"
For illumination "*sans fin,*" fire, ash, incandescence.

Arthur Rimbaud: *Une Saison en enfer*, letters (05/15/1871, 08/04/1888, 06/23/1891)
Paul Verlaine: "*L'Angoisse,*" "*Dans l'interminable ennui*"
Fred Chappell: "Burning the Frankenstein Monster: Elegaic Letter to Richard Dillard"
Henry Miller: *The Time of the Assassins*
Vladimir Nabokov: *Lolita*
Enid Starkie: *Rimbaud*

COURAGE

"*Es steht da,*" it is there, like "*unser Leben,*" all that
Is the case, words, your being able to "accept many
Things," wars, one you fought in, "*vom Wahnsinn*"
Surrounded, madness, three brothers dead, *Selbtsmord,*
Tempted yourself, suffered "*die Schrecken der Hölle,*"
A single day quite enough, instead "*Selbstgespräche,*"
Conversations, Ludwig, often stammered, with yourself,
Silent, locked, where "*man nicht sprechen kann,*"
Yet sure philosophy should be written "*nur dichten,*"
As a poem, spoke like a lion, who could understand?
Today lionized, reviled, revered, explained, imagined,
Abused, outed, puzzle "solved", despite commandment,
"*Spiele nicht,*" don't toy with, "*den Tiefen,*" depths
Of another, whole cloud of philosophy "*kondensiert,*"
Last days, dreams, rain, "*Mut,*" fumbled, now for keys,
Mislaid spectacles, then, finally, face to face, "*das Wort.*"

LUDWIG WITTGENSTEIN: *Über Gewissheit / On Certainty*; *Logisch-Philosophische Abhandlung / Tractatus Logico-Philosophicus*; *Bemerkungen über die Grundlagen der Mathematik / Remarks on the Foundations of Mathematics*; *Vermischte Bemerkungen / Culture and Value*; *Philosophische Untersuchungen / Philosophical Investigations*
The First Epistle of Paul the Apostle to the Corinthians 13:12
Evangelium S. Johannis 1:1

DUST

Years have passed, Cousin Allen (claimed kin, 1964,
So many Virginia cousins), buried you with Confederate
Dead, "grave who counts us," even that poem, "all,"
Once (04/1958) first reading ever attended, Green Drawing
Room, awe, crouched on the floor, piano by the door,
Those different days, now poet behind every podium,
Knocking, "Prospero in steam-heated universities,"
At every academic door, "dull creature of enormous head,"
Lowell mocked *your* "enormous brow," preterist, always
Over shoulder, gray thought, agrarian past, "brass bullet
Mold," great grandfather's secure, lock box (11/13/2005),
You refused to salute Il Duce in '36, yet later gave *Pisan
Cantos* Bollingen, Old Adam, ever "punished by crimes"
Of which you, cuz, "would be quit," women, "shadowy desire,"
Lit Biz, unavoidable drink, then late in life, "enduring love,"
Until your own Appomattox, loss, silence, wintry surrender.

ALLEN TATE: "Ode to the Confederate Dead," "Retroduction to American History," "Sonnets at Christmas," "The Oath," "Shadow and Shade," "The Buried Lake"
ROBERT LOWELL: "To Allen Tate II"

LIGHT

Illuminated, "*un semplice lume*," you, Dante, once lost,
Off "*la diritta via*," then found, now needed, millennium
Of continuing inferno, torture, lies, lies, oh lies, "*malvagio
Traditor*," traitors, mass graves, traitors, traitors, bloated
Rivers, language emptied of all meaning, rank deception,
Heated sour air, bombs ● bursting ● bursting ● bursting,
Betrayers chewed in each, "*ogni bocca*," hellish mouth,
But, dead, still get around, H., baked organs bottled,
Juggled in Kremlin, "one-ball business," M., bald head
Pounded like punching bag, strung up, dug up, boxed,
Bent double, planted again, again, S., too, laid stiffly out,
Then, Moscow night, hurried out of sight, not out of mind,
"*Una selva oscura*" indeed, and every day keeps coming
Down, there, here, pot-belly *Führer*, porcine *Duce*, weird
Sisters at their brewing, need you now, *maestro*, now,
Reshape penumbra, now, into lasting shape of light.

DANTE ALIGHIERI: *Inferno, Paradiso*
SERGIO LUZZATO: *The Body of Il Duce*
RON ROSENBAUM: *Explaining Hitler*
WILLIAM SHAKESPEARE: *Macbeth*

FIRE 2

"Hour of the wolf," you once thought, "now ended,"
But you were, your words, "doomed from the start,"
From first move, fourteen, already crazy, **fool &
Smartest kid in the class,**" testing, Jim, testing
Everyone, "played games," cruel, manic, self-absorbed,
"All the time" suffering, aware "all games contain,"
First move to last, "idea of death," hunted for "good
Disguise" to, J.v.S., "conceal all knowledge,"
Found "drugs sex drunkenness," celebrity, fame,
"Wasted" ● "Broken" ● "Rock & Roll Wars,"
It was poetry you wanted, "always be a word-man,"
Notebooks, poems, "leather lamb," dreamt of "sorrowful
Poetic con-man," dark Africa, Rimbaud, "Mr. Mojo Risin',"
Then, "fucked up," ended up, "can't stand it anymore,"
Making your last move, Paris grave, graffiti "gloomstone,"
James Douglas, no other words, "pissed it all away."

JAMES DOUGLAS MORRISON: "Jamaica," "Lamerica," "As I Look Back,"
  The Lords: Notes on Vision, "I dropped by to see you," "Drugs sex
  drunkenness battle," "Untrampled Footsteps," "Cold electric music,"
  "An American Prayer," "Dry Water"
JERRY HOPKINS AND DANNY SUGARMAN: *No One Here Gets Out Alive*
JOSEPH VON STERNBERG: *Fun in a Chinese Laundry: An Autobiography*
PATTI SMITH: "death by water"
JACK KEROUAC: *On the Road*

DOUBT

Nature, "careful of the type," Alfred, "so careless
Of the single life," yes, "Nature, red," you knew,
"Tooth and claw," so aware, "body come from brutes,"
Those "lower pleasures," Huxley said you "understood
The drift of science," Lyell, eventually *Descent*,
T. S. E. called you "saddest of all English poets,"
Those "grave doubts," grinding down, dust to dust
To dust, smug biologist, TV (12/14/2005), hyping book,
Claims Darwin "better poet" than you, so it goes,
Poets do "have a pretty hard center," but you feared
That "I shall pass, my work will fail," said words
At best "half reveal, half conceal," only "murmurs
From the dying sun," and yet "old worn weary,"
Watched, "The Bard," spirits (04/18/1888) twirl table,
Chided giggling girls, sought, raps and taps, still
To know "how fares it with the happy dead."

ALFRED, LORD TENNYSON: *In Memoriam* LV, LVI, XLVIII, LVII, V, III,
    XLIV, "By an Evolutionist," "Locksley Hall"
THOMAS HENRY HUXLEY: Letter to John Tyndall, 10/15/1892
T. S. ELIOT: *"In Memoriam"*
C. DAY LEWIS (AS NICHOLAS BLAKE): *Head of a Traveler*
E. O. WILSON: Interview, *The Charlie Rose Show*, 12/14/2005
EDGAR ALLAN POE: "The Raven"
ELLA COLTMAN: "VISIT TO FRESHWATER | April 1889 [sic] | (Ella
    Coltman's journal)" [misdated 1889 when internal evidence shows it
    to have been 1888]

EXILE 3

"Go on too far," you found out, both, "to find
A grave," Charles, 89, Dick, 100, go "mostly alone,"
Ever alert, "senses shook," to silent architecture
Of "unmarked bones," such full lives, tutor, Dick,
Prajadhipok, gunnery instructor, professor, poet,
Charles, "poet, sergeant, Under Secretary," honored,
Dick, Bollingen, Pulitzer, Poetry Consultant L. of C.,
Signed book (04/24/1961) from "~~George~~" to "~~George~~,"
Then (06/16/2005) "CENTENARIAN POET WHO OUTLIVED
HIS FAME," Charles, Companion of Honor yet "relic
For whom end does not arrive," your "Tristia" reduced,
New Directions, to "Trivia," seeing only, like Orpheus,
"With what ineptitude," looking back, "course was run,"
Said you wished, Dick, to live "at the pitch that is
Near madness" but discovered "disindividuating Chaos,"
Cold waves that slap the empty Pontic shore.

C. H. SISSON: "On a Favourite Death," "The Way," "Finale," "Et in
    Arcadia ego," "Tristia"
RICHARD EBERHART: "The Groundhog," "'If I Could Only Live at the
    Pitch That Is Near Madness'," "The Passage"
EDWIN ARLINGTON ROBINSON: "The Man Against the Sky"
ANDREW ROSENHEIM: "Centenarian Poet Outlived His Fame,"
    The Independent, 16 June 2005
M. L. ROSENTHAL: "Foreword to C. H. Sisson's *Selected Poems*"
PUBLIUS OVIDIUS NASO: *Tristia*

POETRY

"Dotes on poetry," mother wrote (12/1896) to "perfectly
Horrible degree," you, at Bryn Mawr, "writing is all
I care for," Marianne, & later, precise observation, stacks
Of *National Geographic*, writing, "fiercely ambitious,"
Not poems, "exercises in composition," in Carlisle,
"James" Thorpe your pupil, Manhattan, your "thread-like
Hand," Brooklyn, again Manhattan, told W. S. you "tried
Not to rise" above "conversational level," yet "complete
Disintegrator," he said, "equally complete reintegrator,"
W. C. W. called you "leading light," you found his poems
Vulgar, "of the Sex of the Future," shy, sharp-eyed, alert,
Had, "neat and hard as an ant," the wisdom to scissor,
"Strict duty," unnecessary toad from unnecessary
Garden, to know, on way to zoo, or to the grave,
Must always go, "as if, as if," carapaced, to see, "thick
Skin be thick," always, "it is all as ifs," the elephant.

MARIANNE MOORE: statement in "Some of the Authors of 1951 Speaking
    for Themselves," *New York Herald Tribune Book Review*, 7 October 1951;
    "'Am I a Brother to Dragons and a Companion to Owls?'," "Poetry,"
    "Elephants," "Melancthon"
BONNIE COSTELLO: "Tribute: Marianne Moore" (11/06/1997)
WALLACE STEVENS: Letters to Barbara Church (05/06/1954 & 06/26/1952),
    Letter to T. C. Wilson (03/25/1935)
WILLIAM CARLOS WILLIAMS: Letter to Marianne Moore (02/21/1917)
JOHN M. SLATIN: *The Savage's Romance: The Poetry of Marianne Moore*
TED HUGHES: "The Literary Life"
GEORGE GARRETT: *Going to See the Elephant*

NIGHT

Beaten, night after night, flogged, roughshod friars,
Seventeen nights, *imitatio Christi*, composing,
Memorizing, *Cántico espiritual*, "the ways of love,"
Noche oscura, Popes, *Führers*, warrior presidents,
Always "*guerra*," secret courts, sessions, Star Chamber,
"Determined complaint is founded," lies, "pattern"
Of lies, "evils can now measure," "*vida terrena*," here,
"*En escuro*," now, "only by their infinite insignificance,"
And so, "*Doctor Místico*," you, Juan de Yepes, Frey Juan,
San Juan de la Cruz, discalced, caught on Mount Carmel,
Like Vassar Miller (10/20/1963), Monticello's West Lawn,
"¡*Asombro!*," hop, freed fledgling, bright autumn sun,
"Blest bones dance," burning as you burned the letters
Of Santa Teresa, "script as rare as a necklace of ash,"
Ascend, "*no diré lo qui senti*," only "slightest foretaste,"
"*Un entender no entendiendo*," see, beyond light, light.

SAN JUAN DE LA CRUZ: "*Entréme donde no supe*," "*Tras de un amoroso lance*"
SANTA TERESA DE JESÚS: "*¡Cuan triste es, Dios mio...!*", "*En la cruz esta la vida*"
HENRI MEILHAC AND LUDOVIC HALÉVY: Libretto to Jacques
　　Offenbach's *La Périchole*
JOHN MCTAGGART ELLIS MCTAGGART: *The Meaning of Existence*
JORGE GUILLÉN: *Cántico* – "*Más allá*"
VASSAR MILLER: "My Bones Being Wiser," "A Dream from the Dark Night"
RENÉ FÜLÖP-MILLER: *The Saints That Moved the World*

EXILE 4

White man, "BRRRRRRIIIIIIIIIIIIIIIIIINNG!" listen,
The Bantu, shivering in long dream, saved, SAVED,
So new to them, window, door, & you, Richard, lost
First to fame, "god that failed," then France, & you,
Melvin, exiled from birth, in, "Eliotic bones," USA,
R., recall nausea (01/27/1961), Bigger at the furnace,
Aghast that morning, "there ain't a thing we can do,"
R. & M., "White and not-white dichotomy," hung
Out, "black outsiders," to dry, "brand-new $-world,"
M., sought "clarity the comma gives the eye,"
Despised *"howl-howl-with-the-combo* quacks," yet
Also knew those who can't do, "weeping monkeys,"
Theorize, "Critics' Circus," finally, not unlike E. P.,
Unfinished cantos, *"J'y suis, j'y reste,"* R., novel
MSS. unfinished too, 4,000 haiku, "not ideas,"
Only moon, fog, rain, mist, ice, sun, silence.

RICHARD WRIGHT: *Native Son, White Man, Listen!, The Outsider, The Long Dream,*
"Island of Hallucination," "A Father's Law," *Haiku: This Other World*
MELVIN B. TOLSON: *Harlem Gallery: Book I: The Curator:* "Beta," "Delta,"
"Eta," "Kappa," "Mu," "Upsilon," "Phi," "Chi"
RICHARD CROSSMAN, ED.: *The God That Failed*
ERSKINE CALDWELL: *Trouble in July*
WALLACE STEVENS: "Not Ideas about the Thing but the Thing Itself"

PASSION

Schooled only in ambition, by "shade of Milton,"
George, "Blake large and bright," lauded by Yeats,
"Lovely subtle mind," youngest poet in *Oxford
Book of Modern Verse* (1936), taken up, poems,
Passionate, intense, by T. S. E., Oscar W., envied
By, "should be indecently buried," Dylan Thomas,
You two paired, "Christ and the Devil," until
D. T. dead by drink, and you moved aside
By Oxford wankers, Larkin, Amis & Co., Ltd.,
Barker's "School," Geoffrey Hill to Heath-Stubbs,
Michigan (1960-61), only "Me . . . you," then Sisson,
Higgins, until (03/31/2005) note from bookseller,
"This little rarity," 838 pages, *Collected Poems*,
"At heart anarchic," ars poetica, "poet an enemy"
Of the banal, the "stupid stuff," the deadly "violent
Spinning of things," enemy who sometimes wins.

GEORGE BARKER: *Calamiterror* 6, 8, 9, "Holy Poems ii," *Essays*, "Poet as Pariah"
WILLIAM BUTLER YEATS: Letter to Dorothy Wellesley (09/08/1935)
JOHN PRESS: *Rule and Energy: Trends in British Poetry Since the World War*
DYLAN THOMAS: Letter to Henry Treece (03/1939)
ROBERT FRASER: *The Chameleon Poet: A Life of George Barker*
Note on receipt from G. David, Bookseller (03/31/2005)
A. E. HOUSMAN: *A Shropshire Lad* LXII

PASSION 2

All that passion laid in "the deep conundrum
Of dirt" (12/02/1991), final confession,
"Metaphysics of dirt," stone, "spilt on air,"
Silence that Sisson sought, not you, George,
Chanting, expressive, intense, charming the dead,
Milton, Wordsworth, Blake, Tennyson's distractions,
Brooke, reciting Housman, *Last Poems* in hand,
Jaywalking, unpaid fines, Florida (1974), chatter
Of cockroaches held at bay across bedroom floor,
Long struggle, "moral intensity," passionate
Guilt, fucking your way through ● war ●, through
Peace, woman, woman, "tit-in-the-night," woman,
Also men, "several wives of various," you said,
"Cheerful dimensions," child after child after child,
Commemorations, after child, but "logos" always
"At the heart," *resurgam*, "of all natural facts."

GEORGE BARKER: "Epitaph for the Poet," "The Ring-a-roses Tree,"
    "Poem as Dedication Written at the Waterfall of Vyrnwy"
A. E. HOUSMAN: *Last Poems* I: "The West"
C. H. SISSON: "In the Silence," "A Valediction"
MARTHA FODASKI: *George Barker*
DYLAN THOMAS: Letter to Henry Treece (07/06 or 07/1938)
ROBERT FRASER: *The Chameleon Poet: A Life of George Barker*

PASSION 3

"Mystery of the world," George, "we do not know
What is," yes, Ludwig, "*der feinere Unterschied
Zwischen Schein und Sein*," that "words do not
Deal in truth," that "poetry begins where," belief,
"Philosophical propositions stop," and yet, "*certum
Est*," Tertullian, "*quia impossibile*," Christ nailed
To crudely carpentered cross, "λεμα σαβαχθανι,"
To resurrection, "who are these dummies," Hilda,
"Ogres of a past age, fearful effigies, devils, dolls,"
H., S., "Imperial Mussolini pissing on ruins,"
"Seeing ghost," Gertrude, "of his son-in-law," lies,
Betrayals, lies, all "*l'armée des ombres*," all
"A thing of custom," all a terrible dream, all real, all
Real, porkers mincing down to wrecked seas, shame,
Slaughter, "*vargtimmen*," breaking, chiaroscuro, of light,
Now I ask, *ora*, that you, *pro*, pray, *nobis*, for us all.

GEORGE BARKER: "Letter to a Young Poet," *In Memory of David Archer*
   XXXIV, *Anno Domini*, "The Neo-Geordies"
LUDWIG WITTGENSTEIN: *Zettel*
TERTULLIAN: *De carne Christi*, 5:4
Κατα Μαρκον 15:34
H. D.: *End to Torment: A Memoir of Ezra Pound*
GERTRUDE STEIN: *Wars I Have Seen*
JEAN-PIERRE MELVILLE: *L'armée des ombres*
WILLIAM SHAKESPEARE: *Macbeth*
The Gospel According to St. Matthew 8:32
INGMAR BERGMAN: *Vargtimmen*

EPILOGUE

I can believe, myself, that the dispensations of the heavenly will bend their heads and listen, if they bend them at all, to the supplications of the dead rather than to those of the living. Even that, to some degree, the will of God is — no, not modified, not mollified, but, made, perhaps, a little more human, by the accumulated admonitions of all those who have died. So that we, the living, are, in this sense, indebted to our predecessors for some small mercies.

George Barker
The Dead Seagull

FACTORY
HOLLOW
PRESS

Amherst
Massachusetts